Laryngectomy is not a tragedy

(An introduction to pharyngeal speech)

...ue books

60000 0000 ...

D1437899

4.95

Peterborough City Council

60000 0000 20989	
Askews & Holts	May-2011
617.533	£4.95

The author 23 months after laryngectomy.
On his lapel is the membership badge of the
International Association of Laryngectomees.

IN MEMORIAM

Sydney Norgate who unselfishly and
enthusiastically brought so much hope back
to the lives of fellow laryngectomees died
peacefully at his home
March 1994

Laryngectomy is not a tragedy

(An introduction to pharyngeal speech)

Sydney Norgate

Foreword by

L. F. W. Salmon
MBE, MS, MB, BS, FRCS, MRCS, LRCP
Consultant Throat and Ear Surgeon Emeritus, Guy's Hospital
Past President of the British Association of Otolaryngologists

Published by:- Cancer Laryngectomee Trust.
Printed by:- Reuben Holroyd Print, Halifax.

ISBN 09513091-0,2.

CLARENCE HOUSE
S.W. 1

11th July 1989

Dear Mr Norgate.

I write to thank you for your letter of 6th July which together with the enclosures I have handed to Queen Elizabeth The Queen Mother. Queen Elizabeth is grateful to you for writing as you did and read with interest your book with its kind inscription to Her Majesty.

It gave The Queen Mother pleasure to meet and have a talk with Betty Gibson at the Reception in St. James's Palace, and I am asked by Her Majesty to convey to all those involved in the work of the Cancer Laryngectomee Trust her sincere good wishes for the continuing success of your endeavours.

Yours sincerely.

Martin Gilliat.

Private Secretary to
Queen Elizabeth The Queen Mother

Sydney Norgate, Esq.

The 2002 reprint of this book was made possible by the generosity of a legacy from Mr John Bearder MBE and a donation from the Sovereign Health Care Trust.

Foreword

The doctor-patient relationship operates to the advantage of both parties, although the patient rarely recognizes it. Few doctors would maintain their morale without the example and encouragement provided by many of the often seriously ill and disabled people for whom they care. For example, the throat specialist is from time to time faced with the need to confront someone, usually a man in late middle age, with a particularly grim choice; either to accept the sacrifice of his larynx, the principal organ of speech, or to reconcile himself to a long and distressing illness with the probability of a fatal outcome. The majority of such patients, after who knows what agonies of mind, accept the operation and join the ranks of those we call the laryngectomees. Thankfully, the surgeon concerned is supported by the knowledge that almost certainly his patient will come through his surgical ordeal with far less upset than he anticipated, may well return to his job, will almost certainly regain his ability to communicate by speech and, not least, will set everyone around him an example of good humoured fortitude. That this may be expected has been well known for a long time. It is forty-five years since one of the great American authorities on this problem described these patients as 'a most optimistic, cheerful group' and every throat surgeon since has gladly echoed this opinion. If there is a body of disabled patients capable of reviving the weary doctor's faith in the indomitable capacity of the human spirit, it is the laryngectomees.

One such is the author of this book and no one illustrates their characteristics better than he does. If a sense of humour is an ability to laugh at oneself, then Sydney Norgate can claim to possess it in plenty. I hope and believe that this monograph will be read by many with no more than a general interest in the subject and I am confident that these readers will enjoy it without regard to the technicalities. No doubt, however, it will find its way into the hands of speech therapists and other professionals who may feel challenged by two considerations. First, that here is someone, unqualified in this specialized field, setting out to instruct patients in matters that they, the speech therapists, with much experience, are bound to understand better than he does; and second, that a number of his opinions run counter to the generally accepted views concerning the voice after laryngectomy.

Most certainly the author is not a trained paramedical and his choice of language, particularly his way of describing certain anatomical and physiological details, betrays this. However, I hope the specialist reader will not allow this to distract him or her (most speech therapists require the latter pronoun) since there are weighty considerations on the other side of the account. It must not be overlooked that the author has himself experienced laryngectomy and its consequences and that his story has the virtue of autobiography. Moreover it is quite clear to me that he has set about understanding and mastering his disability with a degree of concentration and keenness of observation that is truly remarkable - perhaps unique. The experiments with the whistle and blowing up a balloon, for instance, are new to me and worthy of careful objective study. I hope someone will undertake this.

But there is another point needs making also in this connection. For more than sixty years it has been recognized that while many patients after laryngectomy acquire spontaneously the ability to produce voice, often with remarkable success, others do not. The first suggestion that these others could be expected to benefit from a definite course of vocal instruction came from W. W. Morrison in the USA in 1931 and now the pendulum has swung to a point where it is commonly supposed that no laryngectomee can be expected to make progress without such help. Sydney Norgate does well to remind us of what every laryngologist knows, that is of the tendency for the laryngectomee to acquire voice in the way that the infant does, not by being told how to but by discovering how to.

I have heard that his advocacy of my suggestion that it is misleading to call his voice oesophageal has exposed him to the scorn of the orthodox. I am sorry. It has always seemed to me that 'oesophageal speech' is a misnomer even in the case of those many laryngectomees who produce it after swallowing air so as to produce sound by eructation. All of us happily normal speakers produce voice with air forced through the vocal cords from the lungs but we do not call this pulmonary speech. The vicarious vocal cords, if they may be so called, that produce sound in the laryngectomee are somewhere in the depths of the pharynx. However, in the case in question, it seems unlikely that the oesophagus plays any part at all and this is why the pharyngeal speech of Sydney Norgate needs special investigation.

I have praised laryngectomees for remaining cheerful and resolute in adversity and gratefully acknowledge the debt their doctors owe them, but there is a third reason why they deserve praise and thanks. They play an essential part in the management of laryngectomees-in-prospect.

Consider these events. The case has been diagnosed, the facts have been laid before whoever is nearest and dearest and then, with all possible compassion, the patient has been told the facts and of the decision he must make. His imagination fails him when he tries to grasp his circumstances after the operation and he is fearfully inclined to give up the struggle and resign himself to the end. This is when the surgeon-in-charge turns to his panel of trusted allies, one of whom can always be relied upon, at this critical moment, to stem the tide of despair, provide reassuring answers to most of the doubts and help the patient to find the courage to say yes to surgery. He asks for a volunteer, from among those patients who have already trodden this painful path, to visit the patient and comfort him with reality. This intervention always succeeds and, that it does, is the ultimate tribute to that ebullient and selfless band, the laryngectomees.

The author of this inspiring little book mentions his own rôle in this last respect almost in passing when he tells us the stories of Eddie and Brian, so that it is left to us to form our own assessment of just how much his pre-operative counselling and example must have meant to these two men.

I shall sum up my opinion of Sydney Norgate by stating my belief that he belongs to that breed from which the Douglas Baders of our race from time to time rise up and, although he would heartily and with true modesty seek to deny the comparison, what follows provides, I am sure, moving and convincing evidence of it.

London, 1984   L.F.W.S.

Royal Halifax Infirmary
West Yorkshire, 1982

When I removed his larynx three years ago, Sydney Norgate was sixty-seven and had been used to living life to the full. His infectious enthusiasm and his practical approach to new problems are clearly evident and much appreciated by all who come into contact with him. The most significant part of this personal account of life without a larynx is his unique analysis of post-laryngectomy speech. I am very pleased that his success in overcoming the difficulties of laryngectomy will now be on permanent record for all to share.

R. T. Watson

We both feel that the publication of Mr Sydney Norgate's book will benefit patients having to undergo this type of surgery. Mr Norgate has been a great help to fellow laryngectomees and their families both before and after the operation.

We wish him every success with his book.

G. M. Metcalfe (Nursing Officer)
J. Hopkinson (Ward Sister)

Preface

After laryngectomy, my body reacted to the new conditions in such a remarkable and co-operative manner that I was compelled to record the new sensations, the effect on my fellow men and how speech came to me again. I had been given a second opportunity to experience hopes and fears, aspirations and disappointments and finally the thrill of achievement so often reserved for the young. How wonderful this was compared with the 'second childhood' usually associated with my age group. I do not believe as Alexander Pope suggested that 'life is a long disease' but I do believe that when a person stops struggling, that person dies. What finer struggle could there be than this effort, with nature as a powerful ally, to regain and maintain pride and dignity and become what a laryngectomee should be - a perfectly ordinary person who has a strange voice and breathes differently from most others.

The path to rehabilitation is a joyous adventure and I will never cease to be grateful to the surgeon and nursing staff of Simpson Ward in The Royal Halifax Infirmary who made it possible. As you will appreciate from the text, the surgeon does not remove the sense of humour along with the vocal cords; in fact he removes nothing vital to the patient's needs. If there were leagues for disabilities, then laryngectomy would be in danger of relegation from the Fourth Division once some form of effective speech had been achieved.

I would define as effective any speech which enables communication to be maintained in an intelligent manner. I would quite emphatically place consonant speech as described in the text in this category. With practice it is possible to carry on long conversations using consonant speech. Indeed Brian, whom I had counselled, chaired a business meeting the day after he was discharged from hospital, only four weeks after surgery. Fellow committee members who had expected him to arrive dumb were considerably surprised to find that he was determined to carry on as usual.

Among laryngectomees, I have encountered some disquiet about those who fail to regain speech of any sort in the absence of any physical explanation and I have wondered if the manner of approaching the problem could be the reason. I have found that four days after surgery simple words like 'cheers', 'twitchgrass' or the name of a loved one are well within the capabilities of patients. I believe quite firmly that no patient who speaks at that stage can possibly fail to learn at least consonant speech even if full voice is beyond him. If the voice thus produced can be taped and played for the benefit of near relations, then the joyful ride to rehabilitation will have begun.

On this adventurous journey there is no turning back. Is it possible that sometimes communication has been sacrificed at the altar of a God called Voice for so long that it is too late to recapture the possibility of speech of any kind? In putting this question I aim to focus attention on the plight that my fellow laryngectomees may find themselves in, and hope that my experience will give them hope. On a much more cheerful note I was very amused recently to read that whales breathe in a manner very similar to laryngectomees and wondered if a corollary of this would be the assumption that we laryngectomees are having a whale of a time.

I cannot conclude without paying a tribute to Charles R. Nelson, the American pioneer who conquered silence in 1949 and then helped many others to learn speech by writing an instruction book which is still in use in many parts of the world. I believe that my work is a progression from that book and sincerely

Having a whale of a time!

hope that my efforts will create a worthwhile structure built on the excellent foundation he laid and that professional speech assistants all over the world will find it both amusing and helpful.

Halifax 1984   Sydney Norgate

The Man Who Conquered Cancer

Bob Champion riding Aldiniti to victory in The Grand National at Aintree, fifteen months after being cured of cancer.

Bob says: I wish every success to yourself and laryngectomees all over the world and sincerely hope that this book will assist them to acquire the technique required for speech.

The Man Who Conquered Silence

The author leading in his two-year-old winner, Ziparib, at Haydock Park, months after laryngectomy.

The author says: I may look thoughtful in the photograph but leading in a home-bred winner is more serious than a laryngectomy (at the time!).

Acknowledgements

I wish to record my thanks to the following people and organisations for their help in providing illustrative material used in this book:

Morris of the Yorkshire Post for the cartoons.

Alec Russell for permission to reproduce the photograph of Bob Champion and Aldaniti.

The Literary Trustees of Walter de la Mare and The Society of Authors for permission to use extracts from 'Off the Ground'.

Jim Moran Photography, Halifax.

Provincial Press Agency, Southport.

Yorkshire Post Newspapers Limited, Leeds.

This work is dedicated to my wife, Lucy, who made it all possible.

Contents

Author's Note

Pharyngeal or Oesophageal?
The whole of this book is a factual account of the experiences, experiments and ideas of the author. It has been read for medical accuracy by the very eminent surgeon Mr L. F. W. Salmon and in this connection I met Mr Salmon on August 25th 1982. During our conversation I realised that oesophageal speech, the terminology I had used up to that time, did not describe accurately the speech I had learned and which is discussed in this book. It does appear that the gullet itself plays little or no part in the production of my speech whereas the muscles in the pharynx where this voice seems to originate are very important. On this premise then I suggest that such speech can accurately be described as pharyngeal speech.

1. Introduction

This book has been compiled by a man who traded his voice for his life and found a perfectly adequate alternative way of speaking which allowed him to rehabilitate himself in society.

After a person's voice box has been removed the voice it produced has gone forever. It cannot be recovered and the patient is in the same position as a young baby who can hear speech all around but cannot participate. No-one teaches the baby to speak but by experimenting with sounds produced in the throat and encouraged, usually by the mother, the baby masters the art. In a very similar way, by experimenting with sounds produced in the throat and with the help of a trained speech therapist, speech can be achieved without a voice box. It is a completely different form of speech which gives a great sense of achievement to the owner and the professional helpers concerned.

The patient has one distinct advantage over the baby - he or she knows the words, and the lips and the tongue which have served so well in the past are available to be used as before. The major factor that is lacking is a flow of air from the lungs (see diagrams A & B, pp. 54-55). It is necessary to find an alternative for this and once the patient learns to produce and control a flow of air from the depths of the throat to the lips, then speech can be achieved. Later in this book the author will deal more fully with this most important part of learning to speak but it must be noted that just as no-one actually teaches a baby to speak (it learns) so no-one can teach the patient. The speech therapist can guide and advise, but the patient must experiment until the right sound is made in the throat. That is the end of the beginning.

I must also point out right at the start of this book that, with the best will in the world, not everyone can achieve oesophageal speech. If you find that you are having little success, go back to your speech therapist and ask to be put in touch with other laryngectomees. Advice from other 'speaking' laryngectomees is often the most helpful as they will understand what you are going through. Indeed throughout Britain many laryngectomees have come together to form self-help groups. The governing body is the National Association of Laryngectomees Clubs which is based in London. However there are many branches throughout the British Isles, and there should be one near you. Your speech therapist may also be able to advise you on the various alternative methods of communication, electronic and prosthetic, which are available.

I would say to all other 'lost cord' victims that the fault lies not in the stars but in ourselves if we seem to be dumb.

2. After the operation

When I recovered consciousness in the ward after the operation I immediately reached for the 'magic pad' at the side of the bed and wrote down a message. The attendant nurse answered in a matter-of-fact voice and so I was still able to communicate in some form. Only when we are in danger of being unable to communicate do we realise the vital importance of this function. It is of course the ability to communicate intelligently with each other that makes us different from all other earthly creatures. I imagine that if I had not been able to communicate in some way, I might have retreated

"Any complaints?"

into myself and the effort to establish contact would have become more and more difficult. The expression 'keep in touch' took on a greater significance for me and is a useful phrase to keep in mind.

I continued to use the pad for the first ten days but once my stitches were removed I began to experiment with what I christened my consonant speech. There are hundreds of words in the English language which in the proper context are readily understood without any pronunciation of the vowels between the consonants. Consonants like p, t, k, s, produce their own sounds in your mouth, without needing any voice. Remember, it is your voice you have lost, not your ability to speak. There are lots of sounds you can make without voice. You can still articulate with your lips, tongue and teeth by mouthing the words slowly and precisely. In fact, it often helps to imagine you are explaining something to a foreigner, as this should encourage you to slow down.

Here is an example from my own experience. Three days after leaving hospital (22 days after the operation) I started to drive my car but soon realised that I needed petrol. I pulled up at the next filling station, opened the window and pronounced the consonants 's' and 'x', saying in my mind 'six'. As this was in the days when it was customary to be served at the pump and buy in gallons, the young lady filled the tank with the requested amount, took my money, gave me the change and off I went feeling extremely pleased with myself. As far as that petrol attendant was concerned I was a *normal* customer who had asked quite *normally* for petrol and she would, I am sure, have sworn on oath that she had not that day served a customer who had no voice box!

I used this method of speech in hospital when visitors came to see me, assisted of course by mime and, as a last resort, the magic pad. Conversing with the nurses in this way presented no difficulty at all. If you point at a book and pronounce 'b' followed by 'k', the nurse is hardly likely to offer a bed-pan. Using this consonant method I conveyed to one young woman who brought me a cup of tea at 6.oo a.m. that chimps on television make better tea and her merry laughter assured me that she had understood.

Just what the patient ordered!

One night I was disturbed at 3.00 a.m. by a deep sonorous voice which boomed through the hospital corridors like a sound effect from a horror film. I rang for the night nurse and using consonants only asked. 'Is this man a porter?' As there was no light on, the nurse had been unable to lip-read my question, but she replied 'Is he disturbing you?'

'Tell him to shut up.'

'He is a patient but if he's preventing you from getting to sleep I will ask him to be quiet. He's quite a character.'

I knew immediately the identity of the culprit - a nuisance who insisted on sitting up in bed, night and day, wearing a cap of the type favoured by round-the-world yachtsmen. In my more frivolous moments I imagined him sailing round the oceans of the world on a hospital bed, with a crew from the Department of Health.

Two days before discharge I communicated very successfully with a fellow patient. He was due to go down to the theatre for

Looking for the Cape of Good Hope

Awaiting the call

a minor ear operation and made a striking figure as he stood by his bed. A police sergeant, over six feet tall with short, strong black hair in small natural waves and robed in his white gown, he lacked only a laurel wreath to take the lead in a Roman play. With a theatrical gesture, as if introducing him, I said 'Julius Caesar!' His Anglo-Saxon reply that I shut up about Julius Caesar and remember instead that he was due to go to the operating theatre any minute, made it abundantly clear that he had understood my remark.

A USEFUL DISCOVERY

I had learned that because after the operation it becomes impossible to inhale in the ordinary way, the sense of smell is lost but during my last week in hospital I did a most interesting experiment. It was in the month of June and men were busy with huge greedy lawnmowers cutting the long grass on the expanses of green immediately below the ward. I opened a window and sat by it so that the wind was blowing towards me. I opened my mouth and shut it with the cheeks ballooned and then forced the air down and out through my nostrils. Smelling in reverse! And I was rewarded by the faint but unmistakable and quite delicious scent of new-mown grass! I repeated this experiment with freesia sent to a fellow patient and was similarly rewarded.

Before I left hospital I also discovered that I could expel air through my lips in short bursts - as you do when blowing up a balloon - and while I did not realise at the time the significance of this, it later became very obvious that this is the flow of air that one needs for speech. When I made the further discovery that I could expel air in bursts indefinitely while pinching my nostrils, then I understood what I think is the secret of oesophageal speech, as I will explain later.

One week after leaving hospital I drove my wife to the supermarket and while waiting for her in the car park, I was approached by a former neighbour. With a mixture of consonant speech and mime, I conveyed to her that my voicebox had been removed. I felt like a cat with cream when she told me 'My ex-husband's father had the same operation but he can't speak and you can!'.

PRACTISING CONSONANT SPEECH

Here is a list of words to practise, using only consonants. This list is by no means comprehensive but the words are surprisingly easy. The doggerel is the beginning of a poem spoken by me to a nurse the day before I left hospital and he understood every word.

Judge	Six	Check	Chess	Cluck
Squelch	Chuck	Jock	Quick	Chance
Church	Squib	Chad	Jet	Tap
Squash	Jack	Tuck	Chip	Chalk
Tip-top	Kitty-cat	Pork-chop		

Silly old Syd
Sat on the lid
Of a dustbin one fine day.
Along came a man
With a big van
Who carted Old Syd away.
'Rubbish', said Syd -
He often did,
His mouth full of cinders and dirt.

Selection of words suitable for consonant speech

Chimp	Skit	Lush	Joke
Skittle	Luscious	Query	Catch
Joker	Couch	Cashier	Cheese
Couch-grass	Cluck	Touch	Archer
Coach	Tug	Lurch	Cock

Lurcher	Tot	Totter	Tat
Cocktail	Latch	Lazy	Clover
Tatter	Glaxo	Tit	Lack
Luck	Titter	Lux	Tich
Charlie	Lucky	Glad	Pluck
Gladys	Tip	Plucky	Gladioli
Top	Gee-gee	Glove	Shin
Shingles	Chat	Gas	Chaser
Chatter	Gasket	Click	Gout
Joust	Sugar	Chatterer	Jug
Clock	Juggle	Shoe	Clogs
Jag	Squire	Geordie	Jaguar
Clutch	Jam	Scrub	Climax
Scrubber	Climb	Chow	Jar
Chow-chow	Spout	Jam-jar	Clown
Sprout	Clout	Juice	Stitch
Chip	Juke	Ship	Clue
Clux	Juke-box	Shout	Jumbo
Klan	Squelch	Just	Chuckle
Squelching	Choir	Skip	Splut
Justice	Splutter	Choir-boy	Justify
Skipper	Choc	Judge	Scooter
Choc-ice	Judgement	Squint	Choose
Jolly	Swish	Chick	Quest
Switch	Pluck	Split	Cow
Cow-boy	Question	Past	Skate
Snick	Owl	Quench	Snickle

Cowl	Quick	Pox	Clog
Quickie	Poncho	Smudge	Church
Pick	Three	Rub	Trudge
Church-yard	Spud	Pick-up	Rubbish
She-mozzle	Twelve	Jack	Pool
Pick-up truck	Jacket	Sput	Twit
Pik-cha	Sputnik	Twitter	Squirm
Squash	Twitch	Six	Chuck
Thick	Shush	Mix	Squeak
Shuttle	Squawk	Stupid	Mix-cha
Pas-cha	Sixty	Twitch-grass	Shut
Shut-out	Squee-gee	Thirteen	Shuttle-cock

After your operation you will have to wait until your feeding
tube is removed and you are swallowing food normally before
you can start oesophageal speech proper, but mouthing clearly and
practising your consonant speech will help you to communicate
while you are learning to produce voice again.

3. Starting to speak

I learned to speak in two quite distinct and different phases, separated by what seemed at the time to be some sort of miracle. I was discharged from hospital one Saturday and the next day received a visit from my youngest daughter, who made the following remark, 'Well, dad, we tried unsuccessfully for years to shut you up - it seems that the doctors have succeeded!' I had read that belching would supply air for speech and as I have been able to burp at will from an early age, I did just that and produced, loud and clear, two swear words. I then repeated the exercise but instead of swearing said her pet name, Ros, short for Rosalind, to make amends. Thus the battle to learn to speak again began.

Each morning I bombarded my wife with a series of explosive sounds which she did her best to interpret. These words were either one or two syllable words and presented no difficulty if I produced a burp as the vehicle for each one. However the whole business was most tiring and unpleasant to me and must have been quite unbearable for a sensitive listener.

During the second week when the vicar called in unexpectedly, he found me alone in the house. I think I must have upset him very much with my belching, mouthing and miming for he never again called on us, not even for his usual sherry or to say goodbye when he changed parishes.

I soon found that I was able to say some words without a belch. One notable example was the word 'out'. I discovered that this

Figure 1
Practice positioning is very important - the listener should not be able to
lip-read what the speaker is saying.

word would trip off my tongue and that it was less difficult to say
subsequent words than if I had tried to say the same words without
a preliminary 'out'. 'Out' may not be the best word for you, but keep
trying and you will find a word which you can say easily, and then
you can use it as your starter, e.g. tap, scout, pipe, tip-top.

I experimented by raising my chin high, found that this increased
the volume for some words and when I dropped my chin on to my
chest, some words could not be pronounced at all.

I tried counting one to ten, then to twenty, pausing after each
word, and if I got stuck said the word 'out' in order to get started
again. I also worked on the various vowel sounds:

a	as in	*bat*
a	as in	*Cain*
a(w)	as in	*tall*
u	as in	*chuck*
u	as in	*tune*

i	as in	*chip*
i	as in	*kite*
o	as in	*chop*
o	as in	*coke*
oo	as in	*cook*
e	as in	*cheque*
e	as in	*cheek*

For a week or two I found it quite impossible to say 'i' as in 'kite' but when I did say it, I was surprised to find that my wife had not realised that I had pointed to myself to suggest the word 'I' when I wanted to use the first person singular and she had great difficulty in accepting that I had not actually spoken the word. This gave me a further insight into the business of communication. Provided that the intended meaning is conveyed, you need not be too pedantic or critical about quality or method.

DIFFICULTIES ENCOUNTERED

My normal practice time was in the mornings and before starting I did my 'irrigating'. I cleaned out the tubes and if I still felt a bit stuffed up, I had a steam inhalation which soon cleared all the passages. It seemed that I had to practise when I felt physically strong and when my throat was clear of impediments and food particles. By evening, I usually found it quite impossible to say anything at all, nor could I manage anything when I first got up in the mornings.

My speech certainly did not get a little better each day; it seemed rather like climbing part-way up a cliff and then sliding back, varying distances each time it happened. So many things seemed to affect this new voice I was trying to master: indigestion, catarrh, bad colds and sore throats all make it more difficult to produce oesophageal speech but what makes it quite impossible is tension. I think it is very necessary for the speech learner to learn first of all how to relax and acquiring your own technique is time well spent.

I was lucky enough to learn a technique as a teenager, when idly investigating some abstract religious practices and I am convinced that my ability to relax has played a very important part in my learning to speak again. My method is as follows:

Firstly remember that although relaxation is physical you need positive mental effort to achieve it. Start with your left foot and make it feel weightless. Then work up the leg and relax the muscles. Do the same with the right foot and leg. Now your arms, wrists, hands and finally fingers. If you are able to sit at a table, rest your elbows very gently on the surface but do not press down. Now relax all the neck muscles, cheek, jaw and finally, this is vitally important for our purpose, relax the stomach muscles. Even now after hundreds of telephone calls, I still consciously relax my stomach muscles before picking up the receiver both when making a call and receiving one. Relaxation is very important if the words are to fall from the lips like the gentle dew from heaven.

Before beginning to try to speak I used to sit in the kitchen with my legs square under the table, my elbows resting lightly on it, and then made sure that my whole body was relaxed. Sitting position can also affect your ability to relax. I found when learning oesophageal speech myself that in no way could I relax sitting on a settee or easy chair as both are unnatural positions.

Very gradually I became more ambitious and started to attempt to read newspaper advertisements out aloud to my wife. For some strange reason I found that farm stock sales gave me the most variety and I stammered and spluttered my way through them while my long-suffering wife did her best to follow me. During this exercise, I did not seem to have any more difficulty with long words than I had with short ones, so I then turned my attention to some really long words.

We have in the garden a plant which rejoices in the name of macarantheratanicertifolia and in pre-operative days I used to reel this off to impress visitors. By the 20th August, seven weeks after leaving hospital, I would work my way through this word with no more difficulty than a word like 'umbrella', and much more easily than the word 'uphill'!

4. The miracle

For many years as part of my annual holiday I spent one week in August attending York Races. To test any possible reaction to the noise and bustle of a race meeting I visited Ripon Races on the Saturday before the York Meeting, only seven weeks after leaving hospital. As I had no discomfort driving to Ripon and thoroughly enjoyed the afternoon, I decided to travel the forty miles each way to the York Meeting on the 22nd, 23rd and 24th August. At many a race meeting I have often wished for a miracle, usually when I have backed a second and hoped for an objection or a failure to weigh-in, but this time the miracle happened and it was not to do with racing.

Leaving my wife safely esconced on the lawn, I went to a part of Tattersalls where I knew my farmer friends would be congregating and immediately met one of them, a worthy opponent in many a dour domino battle. 'How are you?' he asked and pointing to my throat I said in a level, pleasant voice, 'I've had an operation on my throat'. No belch, no splutter and absolutely no preliminaries. I stood there and said those words. What is more, we continued our chat until we reached the grandstand and went our different ways. Almost immediately I met another acquaintance and pointing to my throat I told him that I had been 'tubed', the term for an operation performed on horses to cure respiratory complaints. He was very gallant and replied, 'Well, they only tube good 'uns!'.

I was too tired to practise speech when I got home from the races in the evenings and could spare no time in the mornings before setting off, so it was the end of that week before I got back to my kitchen table routine. Remembering my chats at the races, I was very excited as I practised my vowels, the normal beginning to each session.

My elation and excitement were both short-lived. I became quite dejected when I realised that in no way could I repeat the York Races speech. It was at that time that I fully appreciated the agony and loneliness of the long distance runner. Learning oesophageal speech requires many of the qualities of a marathon contestant, and one quality in particular - persistence. There was only one solution and that was to go back to the old routine. My practice ranged widely - vowels, newspaper advertisements, doggerel, poems and counting numbers. However, it was while counting numbers that I made a most startling discovery.

For weeks I had been struggling to take air into the throat, lock it, and then release it in one, two or three syllables of speech and then stop to replenish the air and start speaking again, until the day I successfully counted to twenty-five without a pause. With great amazement, I tried again and went on and on up to sixty, then to eighty, and finally one hundred. The only very slight pauses I made were to replenish the air in my lungs via the stoma to save myself from collapsing from exhaustion. As I counted I was not belching, nor was I gulping in supplies of air. Like a fisherman who senses that any second his float will disappear, I sensed that I was on to something.

I began to wonder where the air was coming from for all these words and parts of words. I concluded that, as I spoke, air must be going up my nostrils to replace the air I had expelled in speech. However, when I pinched my nostrils with my fingers, I was still able to count on and on and on.

I next applied cold logic to the whole problem and suddenly knew how Archimedes felt when he shouted 'Eureka' to the Athenians. It was so obvious once I realised what was happening! By saying number one, I had created the air supply conditions to say number two and by saying number two, I had created the air supply conditions necessary to say number three, and so on until exhaustion. Once air is expelled from the back of the throat by speech - air is present there all the time - then nature (if you recall the physics lessons from all those years ago) abhorring a vacuum, will replenish the supply. We do not need to gulp, gasp like a fish or belch like a drunkard - once we start to speak, nature makes sure we can continue, so long as we have the strength to do so.

I was able to test my theory there and then. Before my operation, I had had great fun with that most demanding of pets, a Jack Russell terrier. I had in fact trained it to come to the call of a referee's whistle. After the operation I was not able to produce long blasts but soon learned to make short toot-toot-toot sounds to which the dog responded (when it wanted to, that is). I now blew this whistle without moving it from my mouth and found that I could go on and on. I pinched my nostrils and sure enough I could whistle and whistle and whistle. The air had only one way to get back to my throat and that was via the whistle itself. If air could reach the back of my throat in the very short time between toots, it was obvious that it could easily do it between the words one, two, three, four, five, six etc.

Before I relaxed finally to wallow in the pleasure of my discovery, I did one more test. Realising that speech was connected with air flow I persevered with practise until I could blow up a balloon.

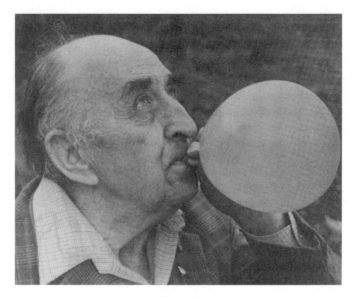

Figure 2
An early achievement was to blow up a balloon, an accomplishment that never
fails to baffle student nurses.

With the lips firmly round the balloon opening, air needed to fill
the balloon had obviously gone up the nose and been expelled
into the balloon in short bursts, with an action similar to the
one used in blowing the whistle. I now blew up the balloon and
with my lips tightly round the balloon opening, I found that
when I held my nose tightly the supply of air was cut off and I
could blow no more. There is of course a hole in the top of a
whistle through which the air can travel back to the throat, but it
is not possible for the air to go back via the balloon.

AFTER THE MIRACLE

Once I had accepted this theory of air supply for oesophageal
speech, i.e. that it replaced air used up automatically without any
conscious effort by the speaker, many things which had puzzled
me became quite understandable.

1. The York Races Miracle. Relaxed in those old familiar surroundings with so many happy memories, I had literally spoken without effort. I had been unable to reproduce it later at home because my brain had been told that I was trying to do something difficult and tension had been present.

2. How, only a very short time after the operation, I could say macarantheratanicertifolia.

3. How a laryngectomee, unable to speak, got snarled up in traffic and unexpectedly said 'Damn!'

4. Why I was able to count up to 100 and beyond without knowingly replenishing the air supply in my throat.

5. As time went on and I could talk more fluently, I found that I could also talk very quickly, which would have been quite impossible had I been gulping air all the time.

6. It also explained why some long words are much easier to say than some short words. One such word is 'squelching'. When pronouncing 'sque' the position of my mouth put air into position to say 'elch'; the 'ch' position of my mouth, in turn, put air into position to say 'ing', thus completing the word. Finally, the mouth position of the 'ng' launched me into the next word!

This discovery did not mean that within a few weeks I had regained full speech and my pre-operative fluency. However, it did mean that I had assumed a completely different approach to the task and I decided to take action to strengthen the muscles in my throat. From then on I started to gargle every night before going to bed. I am not sure that the muscles I use to gargle are exactly the same as the muscles I use for speech but they are in the throat and could in some way be connected. I also took to blowing the dog's whistle regularly and practised blowing up a balloon. Most important of all, I still had my morning sessions sitting at the kitchen table. I practised the vowels at the beginning of each session, as I am sure that they strengthened my voice, but I also said poems I learned as a child, nursery rhymes, poems I had written for my children and the lyrics of popular songs.

It seemed significant that when I was allowed to discard my stoma tube, I was also able to discard the idea of gulping air, as if I was saying goodbye to prescribed constrictions and searching for freedom in a new identity.

TO COPE OR NOT TO COPE

One month later my wife was persuaded by me to visit our daughter, who lives in Greece, for two weeks. Physically my operation had proved an ordeal for her and the worry had been a strain. At first she was reluctant to leave me to look after myself but she finally agreed. I drove her the 25 miles to the airport to catch a 7.00 a.m. flight and then back home to share the house with the dog and the cat. I was quite used to fending for myself, as she had been in the habit of going off on trips to Athens for several years, but this time presented a new challenge.

There is no doubt that supermarkets are a great boon to laryngectomees since all your purchases can be made without saying a word. Consequently it was from such an establishment that I obtained most of my food. I did, however, call on a new acquaintance, a butcher. I pointed to my throat to signify that I had a problem and to concentrate his mind. During my first visit I got along quite well by saying the article I wished to buy and pointed. I felt very pleased with myself and rather mischievously asked my neighbour to let me know if she wanted anything from the butcher's for my next visit.

Although I was very busy during these days, I still made sure I found time to practise. Instead of sitting at the kitchen table talking to myself, I practised speech as I did my household chores.

5. Using the telephone

While my wife was away. I made three successful telephone calls. I say successful because when I had previously tried to speak to the hospital nursing officer on the phone with my wife on the extension in the bedroom, she had been obliged to rescue me and explain what all the grunting and spluttering meant. Now as she was not available, I had to make myself understood or ring off.

Circumstances conspired to assist me because there was a most pleasant reason for the first call. My wife had a winning line on her football pools coupon but before leaving for Athens she had not been able to find out how much she would receive. It was a syndicate win and she was due to collect one-sixth of the proceeds. I knew that I could obtain the information if I telephoned the pools firm after 12.00 noon on Wednesday. I worked it out that I had to say only eight words. When the operator answered, I needed to say, 'Publicity, please'. When the publicity department answered, I needed to say, 'Treble chance dividends, please' and finally, 'Thank you'.

There were two factors in my favour. The nature of the call was so exciting that I could forget my disability and secondly I was making the call for my wife's benefit and did not want to let her down. Years of fulfilling family responsibilities meant that it was easier to do something for her rather than for myself. I prepared thoroughly by sitting at the kitchen table where, after saying my usual vowels, I practised the words I would be using on the telephone. After I had dialled the number, I consciously relaxed my stomach muscles and all went well - so well, in fact, that once I had got the information I asked the young woman to give my regards to her colleague, who was known to me.

Later that day I dialled my daughter's number in Athens. The call was answered by my Greek son-in-law who speaks no English and who certainly was in no position to criticise the quality of my voice. I said 'Lucy', my wife's name, and he called

Figure 3
Using a telephone is no longer a problem.

her to the phone. I had practised numbers so much during the investigation of my theory that I was able to tell her that the win was in excess of seven thousand pounds with no difficulty at all. I then contented myself with answering simply 'yes' or 'no' to her further questions.

These two calls were extremely simple to make but the third was entirely different. It was very, very difficult and I nearly botched it. Learning oesophageal speech is like gardening, an endless adventure. All the time there is something new to try, some new topic to explore and for ever experiments to make.

For a real test I wished to call someone, not a relation or close friend, but someone to whom I was known once I introduced myself. I decided that the young woman who worked as a nanny for one of my daughters was the ideal person. She had been to my house for lunch once since the operation, so had heard my utterances and would not therefore be scared by the sound of my voice. This time I did not rehearse or practise what I intended to say. I dialled the number and she answered, 'Hello'. I had forgotten to relax my stomach muscles and when I opened my mouth nothing happened. I panicked and was about to ring off when she said, 'Hello' for a second time. I swallowed saliva, sighed, relaxed my stomach muscles and said 'Hello Julie - do you know who this is?' I realised afterwards that I should have said something positive instead of disturbing her afternoon's peace with a strange voice asking foolish questions. There was a long pause and I felt myself beginning to panic when, bless the girl, she said, 'Yes, it's Carole's dad'. The rest was easy. I explained that I was learning to use the telephone and did my best to thank her and make her feel important. As for myself, I felt like a king.

From that time onwards I used the telephone whenever I needed to. Only occasionally did I find that people had difficulty understanding me. If I anticipated any major problems I would ask my wife to make the call and warn the recipient that I had an unusual voice, before I proceeded. I have made hundreds of telephone calls since those first three calls and it does appear that an oesophageal voice comes over the telephone very distinctly. One of my acquaintances to whom I had not spoken for some three years (pre-op. days) described it as very effective.

LISTENING PLEA

Do not assume that if you have trouble speaking on the telephone that it is necessarily your fault. The world is full of semi-deaf people who do not seem capable of listening properly. One professional man I called asked me to speak up and complained rather testily that my voice was faint. I replied in a matter-of-fact way, 'My voice is suffering from the fact that I have no voice box, but if you listen carefully you will hear'. He was most apologetic and heard the rest of the conversation without difficulty, not because I spoke any louder or more clearly, but simply because he was jolted into listening properly.

I have been considerably surprised at the number of people who have admitted that they had impaired hearing when I have challenged them because they could not understand what I said. One such person was a press reporter, a quixotic choice by the editor.

BREATH CONTROL

Speaking on the telephone taught me one lesson very important to all laryngectomees. It is to do with breathing and speech. I found that after I had spoken to any of my daughters on the phone for a couple of minutes, I was utterly exhausted and had to pass the phone to my wife. Fortunately I worked out the reason. A normal person has got to breathe in air to speak, both on the phone and in normal conversation, but we are different. I found that because I did not need the breath for speech, I was forgetting to breathe! It's a wonder I didn't pass out sometimes, both on the phone and off it. I think that one of the causes of this unfortunate habit was the fact that in the early days of learning words, I cured myself of making stoma noise by breathing *out* very gently before I said the word, so that there was very little air in the lungs which could cause stoma noise. As a result I had got into the habit of speaking with very little air in my lungs and I was actually forgetting to breathe. I would therefore recommend other laryngectomees not to breathe out completely. My conversational speech has benefited greatly from this discovery and I am able to carry on conversations for some considerable time now without excessive fatigue.

REACTIONS AND RESPONSES

One lady I telephoned accused me of being her young brother disguising his voice to scare her; another girl screamed for her brother to come and take the call; and one dear thing insisted on giving me a prescription for honey and brandy which would cure my throat in no time at all.

The strangest telephone story I heard concerns a laryngectomee who told me that he was thinking of ordering one of the old-fashioned upright phones so that he could put the ear-piece beside his ear and the mouthpiece near the stoma from which he was convinced his oesophageal voice came! This may seem quite ridiculous, but for sixty years he had been used to using breath from his lungs for speech. I myself find that it is quite impossible to decide which throat sensations are actually in my 'swallow throat parts' or in the place where the stoma ends internally. I certainly get the impression that air is going up my nose and into my throat, when in fact it is going through the stoma. This sensation continues even when I firmly pinch my nostrils which makes it abundantly clear that no air can possibly pass this way and yet the sensation persists.

Finally, once you are proficient at using the telephone, don't blame yourself every time if you are misunderstood. I was talking one day on the phone to a plumber in connection with the replacement of a pump in our central heating. I told him that I had in fact bought a new pump but was unable to fit it. 'What sort of a pump is it?' he asked. 'God knows', I answered and to my amazement he said, 'Good, I can fix those!' It seems that there is a make of pump the name of which corresponds roughly to what I had said and the misunderstanding was due to that fact. It had nothing to do with my oesophageal voice and literally could have happened to anyone.

6. Using a tape recorder

Four months after the operation, I bought a tape recorder and found it most useful. This purchase meant that I could practise at any time of the day and without the hitherto indispensable aid of my wife. I would venture to suggest that for someone living alone, it is practically impossible to become fluent quickly in oesophageal speech without such a machine.

My first exercise with it was to repeat my vowel sounds into the microphone and I was astounded to find that when I played the tape back, my voice was reproduced very much like my pre- operative recorded voice. I am not alone in this opinion. My wife and four daughters all remarked on the similarity. I found this most encouraging and I think it was at this stage that I felt that at last I was beginning to talk once again.

I had no regular pattern for using the tape recorder but I recorded the date when I practised, so that I could rewind the tape and listen to how I had spoken on a previous occasion. These recordings did not get better in strict chronological order; some days I was in good voice, others not so good. I found, however, that even if I had heavy catarrh or particles of food in my throat that I could produce speech of some kind. This state of affairs has continued to this day and my wife assures me that she cannot tell the good from the bad. I think perhaps the speech is physically harder to produce under some circumstances, but the result is very much the same.

A year later - eighteen months after the operation - I found a most exciting use for the tape recorder, in fact two uses. I had by then found that I could record and play back a very acceptable voice, so I made use of it at my youngest daughter's wedding.

It does seem that eating and drinking have different effects on the speech capabilities of laryngectomees and I find it impossible to speak with food in my mouth. Moreover I have an unfortunate habit of retaining some pieces of food in my throat. I actually accused the specialist of obeying a government directive to make food go further when he did my operation. In view of this problem I wondered how I could enjoy a wedding breakfast of gastronomic delights and still be in a position to say the suitable words expected of a father on such an occasion. I decided therefore to record the speech on tape and play it back at the appropriate time. In addition, I took a course of decongestants at the beginning of the week so that I might be free of catarrh. After writing and learning the speech, I proceeded to record it. This was no easy task as I had to say the whole speech at one go to avoid punctuating the recording with clicks and pauses as I stopped and restarted the spool. However, I eventually managed it and was pleased with the result. On the day of the wedding I was able to settle down to enjoy the celebration meal, reassured by the presence of the tape machine placed on the table in front of me.

At the appointed time, completely relaxed, not a trace of food in my throat, I was able to stand up and explain to the guests why I had decided to record my speech. Then I reached over and pressed the 'start' button. I believe that the surgeon who had performed my operation would have been proud if he had been there to listen to my performance.

I reflected later that the absence of food in my throat was due to the copious draughts of beer I had drunk. The beer served at the restaurant was guaranteed to give me indigestion so I had obtained permission from the management to take along a six-pint can of my favourite bitter. There is no doubt that the beer and the tape together ensured that I enjoyed the function immensely, but the message for laryngectomees is loud and clear - by making the tape I had removed completely any tension about the speech and so remained relaxed. Only when completely relaxed is it possible to produce acceptable oesophageal speech.

Spurred on by the success of the tape at the wedding, I decided to make another one. I knew that there would be a small party on Christmas day for the ward staff at the hospital where my operation had been performed. My wife kindly made them a Christmas cake and when I delivered it on Christmas morning, I left them the tape recorder so that my message could be played at their gathering. The recording began: 'The voice on this tape comes to you by courtesy of the Simpson Ward of the Halifax Royal Infirmary and was made possible by a laryngectomy performed with great skill...'

One of the nurses who heard it told me afterwards that it moved her to tears and I am sure she meant it in the nicest possible way.

7. Dealing with people

I was very lucky when I first started to speak again for I coined a phrase which has well stood the test of time and still serves me well. It is almost certain that if you open a conversation with strangers by saying, 'Excuse me - I have a voice problem' you will get a sympathetic hearing, especially from children and teenagers.

I did make one mistake with some young kids when I remarked that I only needed one further operation and I would become 'a bionic man', a superhuman character from a television series popular at the time. This description backfired because the youngsters believed me and soon we had dozens of them congregating at the garden gate hoping to get a glimpse of me! One cheeky little devil called out and asked if my father was a frog!

The 'bionic' man.

Very young children seem to find adults quite strange in any case, so one with a hole in his throat and a croaky voice is only marginally different from all the rest and most certainly not worth a second thought

When I first started to practise speech, I realised that I needed someone in addition to my wife to listen positively to me, so I approached the young man next door. When I told him, with considerable difficulty as was normal during those early days, that I was having to learn to speak by belching up air, he told me a most extraordinary story. As young adults, he and some friends had the hobby of rebuilding old Land Rovers and found many reasons to celebrate at the garage where they carried out the repairs. Having consumed a vast amount of beer, one of their favourite pastimes was seeing how many words they could say on one drunken belch! From memory he thought the record was 'God save our gracious Queen'. At least they were patriotic!

The pioneers?

This story gave me added confidence and each day I used to get him to listen to me before I set off on my two-mile walk with Brandy, my Jack Russell.

Figure 4
The restoration of normal active life was my goal after the operation.

PUBLIC ATTITUDES

Many adults think that because we have a speech problem we must perforce be deaf. I remember one hospital visitor who instead of speaking to the laryngectomee, wrote messages on the magic pad. In the hope of getting his visitor to speak, the patient wrote on his pad 'The operation has not affected my hearing'. The visitor nodded benevolently and wrote in reply 'That's good!'

Some adults seem to believe that the operation will in some way have affected the brain and adopt a kindly condescending attitude, but they are not nearly as annoying as the insensitive few who jump in half-way and finish the sentence for us - usually wrongly! The only advice I can offer for dealing with these two categories is simple - *avoid them*.

When eventually the day comes that you start to speak, albeit haltingly, you are very likely to believe that it is your fault if you are not understood, although of course the listener may be deaf and you should not be afraid to suggest it. You will be surprised how often you are right!

I have found that the best listeners are policemen, shopkeepers, shop assistants, pub landlords and bar staff. These people are trained listeners and in our multiracial society have more difficult things to unravel than oesophageal speech. If you are experiencing difficulty in being understood, do not attempt to shout, as this is self-defeating.

You will find that the volume of your voice is considerably diffused in the open air and at such events as public functions, race meetings and soccer matches you will experience some considerable difficulty in making yourself heard. It might be wise if you are going to such an event to consult your speech therapist, who will be able to advise you on the use of an amplifier. There are many of these gadgets on the market today. If you ask at your speech therapy clinic you may find that they will be able to loan you an amplifier for a day if, for example, you have to make a speech, or are attending a public function.

In the next and final chapter, I intend to give you hints and tips on oesophageal speech. You will be given assistance but remember that 'The Lord helps those who help themselves' - a slogan that you should take to heart unless you are an incorrigible shoplifter.

8. Hints and tips and my timetable

1. As soon as you are rid of your stitches, start to use consonant speech. Remember this enabled me to buy petrol just three days after leaving hospital.

2. You will have to wait until your feeding tube is removed and you are swallowing foods normally before you can start oesophageal speech proper. But mouthing clearly and practising your consonant speech will help you to communicate while you are learning to produce voice again.

3. Remember that no-one can teach you to speak again. You must teach yourself in the same way as a baby teaches itself.

4. You are not trying to get your old voice back. You are acquiring a new one.

5. All the speech apparatus is intact except the vocal cords and air flow. You have got to arrange the new air flow, thereby enabling the muscles in your throat to produce the voice.

6. The easiest way to arrange this flow is by belching. If you can belch and have practised consonant speech, then you should be able to speak simple words and perhaps even phrases such as 'God save the Queen'.

7. If you cannot belch (and many people find it very difficult) then you must use the air which is permanently present in the back of the throat.

8. Stay completely relaxed. If you know someone who has knowledge of relaxation, ask them to explain it fully to you and hand on any advice or useful techniques. You cannot learn oesophageal speech if there is tension.

9. There are some words which, if you have mastered the consonant sounds, will force this air from the back of your throat and nature will replace it as quickly as you use it. I can speak as quickly with oesophageal speech as I could in pre-operative days when I was a life assurance salesman and, like Winston Churchill, earned my living with my tongue and my pen.

10. Suitable words will vary from person to person. The following are only suggestions and if none of them suit, search about in the English language until you find others:

Squelch	Judge	Scratch	Church
Budge	Paper	Chuck	Jack

11. **This is very important**
    Breathe out very gently so that there is no surplus air in the lungs to come rushing up to make a terrific stoma noise. Keep relaxed. Speak one of the words shown above.

12. If you don't succeed, keep trying until you find a word you can say.

13. Once you have found a word you can say properly, repeat the exercise. Breathe out gently - relax - speak. Breathe out gently - relax - speak. Breathe out gently - relax - speak. Do this dozens of times. You are using muscles you may not have used before.

14. Strengthen the muscles by blowing up a balloon, blowing a whistle and gargling, but not all at the same time! Your physiotherapist or speech therapist will also be able to advise you on specific exercises which you can do to help your neck muscles.

15. Once you have mastered one word, practise others and try those listed in this book under the heading 'Consonant Speech' (pp. 8-10).

16. You have now changed from a mute, which was how the operation left you, to someone who has started to speak again.

17. Practise these consonant speech words every day for not less than half an hour and every day at the end of your self-imposed lesson, try to say any of the vowel sounds which appear in the book. Follow this rule always:
Breathe out - relax - speak.

18. You will find that these vowels are more difficult than the consonants but once you are able to say them, you have won. You have acquired an oesophageal voice.

19. Don't try to sound the letter H. In some parts it's presumptuous to use it anyway!

20. Remember you don't need breath to talk but you do need it to retain your senses, so remember to breathe, especially when using the phone.

21. Practise counting numbers from one upwards. See how many you can say with voice. It's good fun once you get going. Try to reach one hundred.

22. Every time you are troubled by stoma noise, reduce the air in your lungs before you start to speak. It is surplus air rushing out which causes the noise.

23. Using the technique I have described, all the effort is concentrated above the stoma.

24. I hope you find success and that your new voice will be much admired.

Good Luck!

MY TIMETABLE

Operation	11th June 1979
Consonant speech	20th June 1979
Discharged	30th June 1979
Belch speech	1st July 1979
Bought petrol	5th July 1979

Talked to vicar	12th July 1979
Visited Ripon races	19th August 1979
Visited York races	22nd, 23rd and 24th August 1979
Shopping alone	25th September 1979
Spoke on phone unassisted	30th September 1979
Bought tape recorder	10th October 1979
Made tapes for speeches	December 1980
Address to Calderdale Health Authority speech therapists	31st May 1981
Address to Humberside Laryngectomy Club	4th May 1982

Never from the 20th June when I started my consonant speech could I have been described as a dummy. I repeat - the fault lies not in the stars but in ourselves if we laryngectomees are dummies.

9. Sharing my experience - some other case histories

In October 1981, there was an article in the Yorkshire Post in which my beliefs and theories were explained. As a result I received correspondence on behalf of two interested readers, Jack and Dave.

JACK

Jack's wife wrote as follows:

Dear Mr Norgate,

On reading your article in the Yorkshire Post this morning I felt I must write to you for help for my husband.

He had his voice box removed thirteen years ago. He went to learn to talk but no luck. He now speaks in a whisper but cannot blow a match out. Can you help? My husband is 75 years old.

I was considerably taken aback when Jack and his wife arrived to see me the following Sunday. His wife was incurably deaf in one ear and Jack's attempts at speech were quite unintelligible to begin with. However, his wife, using her good ear, some lip-reading, and a huge helping of wifely intuition acted as interpreter - and his story unfolded.

After laryngectomy Jack had attempted to learn to speak and had acquired the diction he still used. After eleven months without help, speech therapy became available and he attended lessons.

He was taught to belch up air to be used for speech but his G.P. and wife found the whole business so distasteful that Jack was persuaded to revert to his original method which by then his wife could interpret. In this way he had carried on for the next twelve years.

It was after a cup of tea that I began to make some sense of Jack's utterances. As he became less tense I could hear very faintly what I call consonant speech, but it was completely drowned by the sound of air rushing violently out of his stoma.

Poor Jack, for thirteen long and often very frustrating years he had been trying to use the air from his lungs to make oesophageal speech. He had tried to continue using his pre-operative voice which, sadly, surgery destroys forever. He had not understood that the old breathing pattern must be ruthlessly broken. Very slowly and very emphatically I explained to him that the only air available for speech was in his mouth and at the top of his throat. Holding my hand out from my neck just above the stoma I explained carefully that nothing below my hand could influence my speech and finished by telling him that if it were possible to cut off my head at that point without killing me, then I would still keep on talking. By this time Jack was an interested listener and most co-operative when I took him into the kitchen, leaving our wives chatting in the lounge.

We sat at the kitchen table where I had learned to talk and after I had switched on my tape recorder we began: 'Breathe out from your stoma and, without taking in any more air, say squelch'. He said it beautifully and it was music to our ears. I then went through the words I have listed on pages 8-10 and he said every one. He had an excellent consonant voice which was not surprising as he had been using it for thirteen years, but drowning it out with stoma noise. Before switching off the tape I introduced his wife's name, Alice, which he had not used since before his operation, and he made a very recognisable attempt at it. We then rejoined our wives and I played back the recording of our efforts. His wife listened with joy and bewilderment. When she heard him say 'Alice', she smiled at Jack and I felt honoured that I had been able to share with them such a precious moment.

Two weeks later they made a return visit and poor Jack had barely got through the door before his wife exclaimed excitedly 'Go on, show him what you can do'. With quite a flourish, Jack produced a whistle and was quickly tooting away with a twinkle in his eyes and all the assurance of the Pied Piper of Hamelin. This time I did not banish our wives and they watched and listened as Jack worked his way through the words listed in this book. With consummate ease he said them all clearly and when we got to his wife's name he said it loud and clear.

After thirteen years Jack was back again among his fellow men - an ordinary chap who just happens to have an unusual voice, which is what all laryngectomees should be. I will let a friend of Jack's have the final word. This is an extract from a letter to me dated December 1981 which gives this friend's view of Jack's progress.

'I have known Jack for a number of years and have seen him almost daily during which time I must say it was with great difficulty I understood his speech. However, I can say with all honesty I now find it much easier to understand what Jack is saying to me.

When he got the whistle it was a joy to hear him blow it and to see his face at the achievement. Also he blew out the taper with no obvious effort. That to me is almost like a miracle and I am certain both Alice and Jack are over the moon.'

DAVE

My introduction to Dave was quite different. He wrote to me saying that he was still in hospital after his laryngectomy, but was anxious to have any details about speech rehabilitation that I could supply. He felt that at 37 years of age it was very important that he should be able to regain speech of some kind so that he could resume a gainful career.

As we lived ninety miles apart I could not call on Dave in hospital so we struck up a correspondence which went on for three long months. During this time Dave coped with stoma trouble and fistulas and was using a nasal feeding tube. Towards the end of this period, I outlined my theory to him by letter as follows: It is not necessary to 'lock' air in your throat for oesophageal speech. Air from the stoma is not used. Relax, breathe air out of the lungs gently and then speak.

I sent him these words to practise: squelch; judge; church; clutch; justice; sex; Jack; check; chew; chin; chow; chu-chin-chow; click; stench; squib; juice; choose; tick; six; tock; clout; juggle; sugar; chi-chi; climax; sprout; chip; charge. In my next letter I told him to add his wife's name, Stephanie, to the list.

Early in March after eighteen weeks and two days of frustration and delay, the nasogastric tube was removed and Dave started to work properly on the words I sent him. He first obtained permission from the medical and nursing staff to do so. I have learned since that in fact he had been secretly practising the consonant sounds very quietly for some time and when the tube was removed by the doctor Dave had caused some surprise by saying, 'From my feet'. This was in reply to the doctor's comment about the abnormal length of the tube and his rhetorical question, 'Where did that come from?'.

It was on Good Friday morning that Dave and I met face to face for the first time. He and his wife had motored down, and brought with them a bottle of wine which accompanied a most enjoyable meal cooked by my wife. The magic of that lunch is an indestructible memory - Dave was talking. Not just a mumbled word followed by an awkward pause, he was articulating clearly and managing short sentences. With the guidance of two letters from myself and no other help of any kind, Dave had taught himself to speak. For good measure, before he left in the evening, Dave blew up a balloon.

I do not claim that I taught Dave to speak again after laryngectomy. I suggested to him a simple method by which he learned adequate speech in a few weeks. To see the system which I had evolved in my mind as I learned to speak put to the test in a practical way and to see such a happy result filled me with satisfaction and a pleasure that still lingers.

PHLEGMATIC FRED

When I first called on Fred at his home, I was in the company of another laryngectomee. Their operations had been performed nine months previously. My friend had learned effective speech, but Fred had not said a word. Could I help?

We were shown into the front room and I persuaded Fred to sit on a dining room chair with his elbows resting on the table after telling him about the importance of relaxation. I explained to Fred that I was going to ask him to repeat some words after me and told him not to worry if nothing came out as it was only his first attempt. We were not successful so I asked him if he smoked and he signified that he did. I gave him my referee's whistle after demonstrating how I toot-toot-toot on it as this requires the same action as puffing out smoke. With great ease he did likewise and smiled broadly as if surprised. No wonder, for the friend who had taken me along, and could himself speak, could not get a sound out of the whistle! When I went through my list of words a second time, Fred said four of them quite clearly: mix, mixture, Jack, bugger. He failed completely on what I have found to be much easier words for most people such as squelch and cheers. I learned later that his drink at the club was 'mixed', the friend who had taken me along was Jack, and the fourth word, he said, needs no explanation. Before I left, Fred promised that he would practise the twenty words on the card which I gave him and I arranged to call again the following week. All this happened nine months ago and I have called on Fred every available Wednesday since that time.

We start with a few games of dominoes. This is Fred's hobby, and he quite happily says the numbers as we proceed and such words as 'knocking' and 'your drop'. When I go through my words he repeats them with various degrees of clarity and can count up to twenty. He can say Alice, his wife's name, and once surprised me by repeating after me, 'Alice where art thou?' On one red letter day when I said to him, 'Repeat, Philip is in bed', (Philip is his son and works shifts) he just looked at me and said in a voice any laryngectomee would be proud to own, 'He isn't'.

All these things happen when I call on him once a week, but between visits Fred speaks to no-one. He has made for himself a comfortable cocoon of silence and all his creature comforts are freely available to him. His hobbies are gardening and dominoes; his social activities are visits to his club where the steward knows that his drink is a pint of mixed. His wife worked in the unspeakable (literally) clamour of textile mills where lip-reading is used. When Fred came home after his operation she soon learned to communicate with him in this manner and so it has stayed until the present time.

However, he has a lifestyle which surely would be the envy of many harrassed inhabitants of the modern world and I would certainly not criticise him for not wishing to make the really enormous effort he would need to exert now in order to change it. I know that when my wife and I call each week it is a happy interlude and we do enjoy our friendly games of dominoes.

EDDIE

At the surgeon's request I visited Eddie in hospital on 29th June 1982 to talk about the laryngectomy due to be performed a few days later. After I had explained what the operation involves, and at his request, I promised that I would help him to learn the technique of voice production. He listened carefully and only Shakespeare could have bettered his final words - words poignant and defiant - 'I'll see this job through if it kills me'.

I kept a diary of my visits and this is a factual account of how I kept my promise to help him with his speech:

4th day after surgery Asked him to make the action of puffing out cigarette smoke. Invited him to blow a whistle - failed. Invited him to say 'ch'. Said this with a lot of stoma noise.

5th day after surgery Invited him to say 'ch' after gently exhaling. Said it with much less stoma noise.

6th day after surgery Took him copy of lecture made to Humberside Laryngectomy Club. Learned that his wife's name was Janet (via magic pad). Told him to breathe out gently and try it. He said

Janet very quietly but very distinctly and repeated it four times before I left. I suggested that he copy out and try to say the twelve words shown in the lecture.

7th day after surgery Said Janet several times and produced a puff of air on the back of his hand when imitating cigarette smoking. Showed me the twelve words he had copied out: squelch, clatter, church, judge, quick, choir, click, trout, skittle, clutch, squib, cheers.

8th day after surgery Invited him to say the twelve words as I said them to him. He said all twelve very quietly. No resonance but all quite clear. He also said 'Janet', 'chick chicken' and tried to say 'out' (no resonance).

10th day after surgery Found that Eddie had worked in a carpet mill so added 'carpet' to the list. He said most of the words on the list but the sound was drowned by stoma noise. I explained why it is necessary to break the pre-operative breathing habit and exhale gently before speaking.

11th day after surgery Nasogastric tube removed. Sat at normal height table on hard chairs and explained what is meant by relaxation. Spent more time on word 'practice'. He said all twelve words plus 'Janet' and 'carpet'. I added despatch-clerk (his previous employment), Webster's Mild (his favourite tipple), also 'six' and 'ten'.

12th day after surgery Went through all previous words plus Lester Piggot (Eddie likes racing) and Dean Clough (his old place of employment). Suggested that he should not breathe at all while actually saying words. This worked well. There was little stoma noise.

13th day after surgery Visited Eddie in presence of speech therapist. Eddie read all the words on his list and I added rubbish, clock, squee-gee, justice, Jack, jacket, quiet, pick, pick-cha, tickle, twitch, twitch-grass. There was moderate stoma noise but he said twitch-grass excellently with a hint of resonance and I suggested that if ever he got stuck when trying a new word, to say twitch-grass and the ensuing word would come more easily. (I used to say the word out.)

14th day after surgery Eddie said all the words spoken to date and I added 'Jack Sprat could eat no fat'. Eddie read these words from a card and of his own volition added 'His wife could eat no lean'. I spent several minutes explaining to Eddie that laryngectomees can speak without breath in the lungs. This ensures that there is no stoma noise.

17th day after surgery I wrote out the following, based on Eddie's previous employment: 'Crossley's made carpets at Dean Clough which was a textile mill. Axminster carpet made on looms was very good but Wilton carpet was more expensive. Tufted carpet was made at Kosset Carpets, a subsidiary of Crossley's'. He had no difficulty with subsidiary, but there was too much stoma noise.

19th day after surgery Discussed stoma noise. Invited him to empty lungs and count one to six, then breathe in and out and repeat the count. There was no stoma noise. Said twitch-grass many times to start strengthening the throat muscles. Also said alphabet, stopping after every fourth letter. Much less stoma noise today.

20th day after surgery Introduced time of day. 1 o'clock, 2 o'clock etc. Then quarter past one, quarter past two etc. Said twitch-grass repeatedly and also gra-a-ss to try to introduce some resonance.

21st day after surgery Asked Eddie to hold his breath whilst we practised all his words. There was very little stoma noise. Tried blowing a whistle. Moved the pea inside, but no toots. Spent some time on gra-a-ss. A slight hint of resonance.

23rd day after surgery Ran through all the words attempted to date, then words picked at random from the morning paper. Eddie made a good attempt at every one of them.

24th day after surgery Went through all the words on Eddie's card. Tried holding breath while speaking. Very little stoma noise. Made a tape of Eddie speaking these words: squelch, clatter, church, judge, quick, choir, cluck, trout, skittle, clutch, club, cheers, Janet, chick, chicken, out, rubbish, clock, squee-gee, justice, Jack, jacket, quiet, pick, pick-cha, tickle, touch, twitch, twitch-grass. When Eddie heard his new voice for the first time he was delighted. We played the tape through for the benefit of the cleaning lady who was suitably impressed and then made the most incisive comment, 'Are those words specially picked to bring out the talking?' What a delightful person she was!

26th day after surgery Took Eddie first four verses of 'Off the Ground' by Walter de la Mare. Updated the first line to streakers.

> Three jolly Farmers
> Once bet a pound
> Each dance the others would
> Off the ground.
> Out of their coats
> They slipped right soon
> And neat and nicesome,
> Put each his shoon.
> One - Two - Three! -
> And away they go,
> Not too fast,
> And not too slow;
> Out from the elm-tree's
> Noonday shadow,
> Into the sun
> And across the meadow.
> Past the schoolroom,
> With knees well bent
> Fingers a-flicking,
> They dancing went.

After studying this for a few minutes Eddie read it aloud to me. He also learned a sentence, 'Chimps on TV make better tea than this rubbish'. Shortly afterwards a nurse arrived with the tea and Eddie was able to say this to her. When she understood and threatened to thump him, Eddie was delighted.

'Three Jolly Streakers' (with apologies to Walter de la Mare).

28th day after surgery   Took Eddie three more verses of poem.

> By Tupman's meadow
> They did their mile,
> Tee-to-tum
> On a three-barred stile.
> Then straight through Whipham,
> Downhill to Week,
> Footing it lightsome,
> But not too quick,
> Up fields to Watchet,
> And on through Wye,
> Till seven fine churches
> They'd seen skip by -
> Seven fine churches,
> And five old mills,
> Farms in the valley,
> And sheep on the hills;

Said all the words and the poem. Practised gra-a-ss.

30th day after surgery   Introduced the following to Eddie.

a	as in	*fade*
o	as in	*cot*
e	as in	*bee*
u	as in	*cup*

Explained that it was necessary to practise these words to obtain resonance. Went through all words and poem.

31st day after surgery   Went through everything we have done since the operation. I then ran Eddie home. He was discharged. Whatever happens hereafter, he can communicate. Eddie is no dummy. Two weeks later Eddie was tooting the referee's whistle.

10. Tailpieces

My mother, who compensated for her lack of formal education by acquiring a vast store of philosophical saws, once said to me 'Never consider you are best at anything. Be content to be one of the best because sometime, somewhere, someone will turn up who is better than you'.

I was reminded of this when I met Jack R., a laryngectomee who made me sound like some sort of dummy. I, who had made a tape for the surgeon to play to student nurses as an example of post-laryngectomy speech; I whose voice had been praised by all and sundry. Jack had his voice box removed at Guy's Hospital in 1969 and had acquired a very good post-operative voice, so good that he didn't need any artificial aid to call 'Time' in his pub.

Jack told me that he was virtually self-taught and that he had surprised the medical and nursing staff by his ability very soon after the operation. He later took an active part in speech therapy for other patients and the highlight of this period comprised teaching an Arab who spoke no English. The Arab's wife who did speak English acted as interpreter while Jack dispensed his wisdom. Sometime later Jack became joint founder of the Jack Hawkins Laryngectomee Club. Incidentally, Jack Hawkins favoured champagne to make himself burp. Any feeling of inferiority I may have had when comparing my speech with Jack's disappeared when he confided to me that he had taught himself to speak using

'Oh dear, they've got the champagne out.'

a method which was practically identical to the method expounded in this book, but twelve years before it was written.

BRIAN

In the Preface I made mention of a laryngectomee who chaired a meeting the day after he was discharged from hospital and only four weeks after surgery. This man was Brian whom I counselled before he had the operation. At his wife's request, she and their teenage son and daughter visited my house where my wife and I put the operation into what we think is a proper perspective. I explained very carefully to Brian my theories of air control and use of the pharynx. Brian was in the intensive care unit for four days but when I saw him on the sixth day, I taped his voice as he said 'cheers', 'Mary', 'David' and 'Sharon'. I lent him my referee's whistle and a list of speech-provoking words.

Two weeks later when visited by a speech therapist he gave a remarkable display of how the body co-operates with the patient on the path to rehabilitation. Using very good consonant speech he invited the lady to sit down and then proceeded to whistle for her benefit. *Not* with the referee's whistle I had lent him. Nothing so mundane. To the complete bewilderment of his audience he sat up in bed with a happy smile on his face and whistled through his lips, loud and clear, less than three weeks after surgery.

Laryngectomy is not a tragedy.

Useful addresses

Cancer Laryngectomee Trust
National Association of Neck Breathers
PO Box 618, Halifax, West Yorkshire, HX3 8WX
Telephone / Fax 01422 205522
E.mail: info@cancerlt.org Web: www.cancerlt.org

The College of Speech Therapists
7 Bath Place, Rivington Street, London EC2A 3DR

The National Association of Laryngectomy Clubs
6 Rickett Street, Fulham, London SW6 1RU
Telephone 020 7381 9993

Macmillan Cancer Relief
Anchor House, 15 - 19 Britten Street, London SW3 3TZ
Telephone 020 7376 8098

Cancer Bacup
3 Bath Place, Rivington Street, London EC2A 3DR
Telephone 020 7613 2121   Scotland: 0141 553 1553

Kapitex Healthcare Ltd
Kapitex House, 1 Sandbeck Way, Wetherby
West Yorkshire, LS22 7GH
Telephone 01937 580211

International Association of Laryngectomees
c/o American Cancer Society
1599 Clifton Road, N.E., Atlanta, Georgia 30329 U.S.A.

Glossary

Feeding tube
(nasogastric tube)
A fine tube passed through the nose via the oesophagus into the stomach, through which the patient takes his food and drink in the early days after laryngectomy, while healing is taking place.

Fistula
In this connection, a leak from the pharynx; a temporary complication occasionally after laryngectomy, due to failure of part of the wound to heal normally.

Laryngectomee
Someone who has had an operation to remove the larynx.

Laryngectomy
The operation for removing the larynx.

Larynx
The organ located at the entrance to the trachea chiefly responsible for the production of the sound of normal speech. (See Diagrams A & B, pp. 54-55)

Magic pad
A convenient device on which the laryngectomee may write messages in the early days after the operation. The message is easily cancelled ready for the next one.

Oesophageal speech
A popular term for the kind of speech employed by the laryngectomee.

Oesophagus
The gullet; the passage by which food passes from the pharynx to the stomach.
(See Diagrams A & B, pp. 54-55)

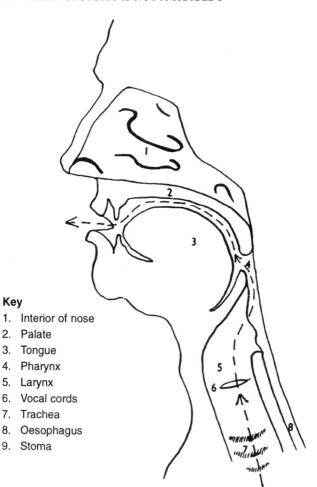

Key

1. Interior of nose
2. Palate
3. Tongue
4. Pharynx
5. Larynx
6. Vocal cords
7. Trachea
8. Oesophagus
9. Stoma

Diagram A

Section through the head to show the nose and throat in a normal subject.

The subject is softly phonating 'ah', a gentle current of air from the lungs being exhaled by way of the larynx (5), pharynx (4) and mouth. Air is prevented from leaving through the nose (1) by the elevation of the soft palate.

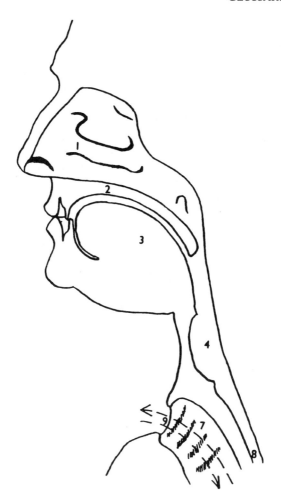

Diagram B

Section through the head to show the nose and throat after laryngectomy.

Note that air passes to and from the lungs only by way of the stoma (9). The nose (1), mouth and pharynx (4) are entirely isolated from the lungs and trachea (7).

Pharynx   That part of the throat into which the nose, mouth, larynx and oesophagus all open.
(See Diagrams A & B, pp. 54-55)

Stoma   Literally 'a mouth', but used here to mean the vital communication at the root of the neck of the laryngectomee through which he breathes.
(See Diagram B, p. 55)

Stoma noise   The noise made when the laryngectomee breathes out hard through the stoma during his early attempts to produce speech. Often at this stage there is an excess of secretions in the trachea, which increases the noise. The author explains the importance and technique of avoiding stoma noise.

Stoma tube   The author's term for laryngectomy tube; a tube made of silver and worn to support the stoma for several days after the operation while healing is taking place.

Trachea   The windpipe; the passage joining the larynx of the normal subject to the lungs.
(See Diagrams A & B, pp. 54-55)